Uriah J. Fields and Malathi K. Sandhu
Photo taken during cruise on the Holland America
MS Amsterdam in 1999

Grandpa Benjamin F. Fields
Chief founder of The Fields School.
He was born in slavery.

The Fields School

An African American School
Without Failures Located in Rural
Alabama 1933-1949

Uriah J. Fields

authorHOUSE®

AuthorHouse™
1663 Liberty Drive Bloomington, IN 47403
www.authorhouse.com Phone: 1-800-839-8640

First published by AuthorHouse 8/27/2009

ISBN: 978-1-4490-0439-2 (e)
ISBN: 978-1-4490-0438-5 (sc)

Printed in the United States of America Bloomington, Indiana

This book is printed on acid-free paper.

THIS BOOK IS DEDICATED TO THE MEMORY OF

Malathi Karuven Sandhu Teacher and compassionate activist whose meticulous research made possible the true story of the Fields School presented in this book.

My parents, Henry and Amanda Fields whose discipline and love gave me the eyes to see grace and heart to feel compassion.

My first and only School teacher the early eight years of my schooling, Clara B. Fields, who inspired me to pursue knowledge.

✦✦✦✦✦✦✦✦✦✦✦

Those who are wise will shine brightly like the brightness of the expanse of Heaven, and those who lead the many to righteousness like the stars forever and ever.

But for you, Daniel, conceal these words and seal up the book unto the end of time. Many will go back and forth, and knowledge will increase.

DANIEL 12:3-4

Contents

Preface   ix

Choosing a Sabbatical Project   xii

The Fields School   1

Introduction   1

The Purpose of this Study   3

Research Questions Addressed in this Study   4

Method   5

Subjects   5

Data Collection Measures Used   5

Fields Family Tree and Fields School students (Listings
from left to right and top to bottom by order of birth)   6

Procedures   9

Summary of Findings of the Study   12

Interview Data from Former Fields School Students &
Teachers   12

The Establishing of the Fields School   14

Fields School Teachers   18

Fields School Teachers and their individual Terms of
Service*   18

Students' Impressions of Teachers   20

Typical Guidance & Discipline used by Teachers   21

Descriptions of the Physical Setting of the School   23

Responses Indicating What was in Abundance at School   24

Things in Short Supply at School   25

What they would Change about the School   26

Fields School Curriculum   27

How Learning and Work were Combined at School   30

Important Lessons Learned at Fields School   31

Life Values Leaned at the Fields School   32

Most Stirring Memory of School   33

What would want for Young Children today to
Experience of Fields School   34

Background Information on Former Fields School
Students   36

Current Residence of Subjects   36

Current Patterns of Residence   37

Education Completed by Subjects   37

Education Completed by Gender   38

Occupations/Careers by Gender   39

Highest Income Earned by Subjects   39

Highest Income Earned by Gender   40

Discussion of Research Questions   40

Student Responses (=26) to What the World Should
Know about the Fields School   41

Conclusions   50

References Cited   54

Other References   56

Appendix   57

Acknowledgments   67

About the Author   69

Preface

One of my greatest privileges was to know Malathi Karuven Sandhu. For most of twenty-five years we were an intimate couple. Indeed, Malathi was "my most significant other." She inspired me to write this prose poem:

My Most Significant Other
My Most Significant Other is one in a million; Maybe, just one among the billions of inhabitants on Planet Earth.
There are many things that are one of a kind; one mother, one father, one of me.
There is also just one Most Significant Other for me.
My Most Significant Other is closer to me than any other human being, preferred by me to any other human being, and loved by me more than anyone else, except for the love I have for myself.
My Most Significant Other, a lover and friend, has no equal or rival."

From "The Saint Troubadour" p. 276

Malathi Karuven Sandhu departed this mortal life in March 2003. One week and one year, respectively, after her transition, in memory of and my connectedness with her I wrote these two elegies:

An Ode to My Most Significant Other

My Beloved Malathi. Your name, in your native India, means flower. Like a flower you were beauty par excellence. Your sudden departure from mortal life has not severed or lessened the bond of love between us.

More than just having pleasant memories of you there is a part of you that is me, no less than the I that is me. I could have never become who I am without you. I learned from you how to love deeply; You helped me to grow and from you I learned how to serve with compassion.

Whatever I have been able to accomplish since we met and will achieve in the future will continue to be for you and me. You remain a tremendous source of inspiration for me.

Surely, you remember this song; you inspired me to write it: I used to sing it for you: "People so seldom say I love you, And then it's too late and love goes away; So when I tell you I love you it's not because I know you'll never leave me, only that I wish you didn't have to go. Now before it's too late let me tell you from the bottom of my heart, I love you. I love you, I love you." And oh how I remember you saying to me time and time again "I love you."

The last words you said to me before your transition were, "I love you too." Your presence and love will never depart from me. We are and will always be Soul Mates. I cannot say to you, "Fare-thee-well" or "Good-bye;"

I can only say to you, my Beloved, "Thank you for your presence and your love."

I love you eternally.

Uriah
(From "The Saint Troubadour", p. 277)

A year later I wrote:

MY AVE FOR MALATHI

One year ago Malathi you made your transition. It happened at a time when it seemed like you had every reason to live. You were vibrant and your life appeared to have been filled with excitement. Indeed, it was exemplary. For your lifestyle was the envy of others who desired, but were not able to muster the courage, to be good to themselves and their own best friends. But suddenly and at the appointed time, a time unknown, certainly to those closest to you, maybe, even to you, or, if known to you, you did not tell us. Or, could it have been we were not listening, at least not well enough to discern the truth about your reality?

Like a flower, which you told me that your name means in your native India, in due season you faded away. Your soul took flight, three days before your breathless and soulless body that no longer could contain it, not even a portion of it, was cremated and the ashes returned to the earth from which they came.

Yes, for a year since you departed this mortal life, I would not, perhaps, could not, let go of you; I could not say farewell. I could only grieve and ache.

Now, one year later, I say, "My Ave for Malathi," not in grief but in celebration. "Farewell, Malathi." Until then... until I join you in that eternal realm where flowers do not die and where souls live forever...I will continue to say as I rejoice these words that I have spoken to you many times while we looked into each other's eyes, "I love you." My Ave for my dearest Malathi.

Uriah

(From "The Saint Troubadour", p. 400)

Choosing a Sabbatical Project

How did it happen that Malathi Karuven Sandhu decided to do a case study on the Fields School?

In 1986, Malathi Karuven Sandhu, director of Mira Costa College's Children's Center in Oceanside, California, spent a year's sabbatical on the Hopi Reservation in Northwestern Arizona, observing Hopi children and their families in school, home, village and ceremonial settings.

Twenty-five years earlier, Malathi had left her native India that she found in certain respects to be like Hopi, especially as it relates to play themes of children as she found in the Hopi Head Start centers and homes.

Malathi was particularly fond of the Hopi ceremonial activities, dances, etc., and the Kachinas (Ceremonial figures).

While she was there I visited her in August when we attended the Hopi "Snake Dance." I was deeply moved by what I experienced. Among other things, it did rain just as the Hopi people believed it would even though no rain was predicted or appeared to be in sight just hours before the Snake Dance. That was a spiritual experience for Malathi and me.

Malathi informed me that Hopi culture like the area in India – North Kerala – where she was raised, is matriarchal and matrilineal. That North India is one of the few areas of India which is matriarchal and matrilineal – the rest of India is patriarchal.

Twelve years later, in 1998, she was about to take a year's sabbatical from Northern Arizona University, Flagstaff, Arizona, where she had been an Associate Professor and at this time Interim Chair of Educational Specialties. She accepted the university president's request to postpone her sabbatical that had been due two year earlier providing her retirement would be granted following her sabbatical.

Malathi considered returning to the Hopi Reservation which she loved so much to fulfill the requirements for her sabbatical. She discussed this possibility with me as well as pursuing a sabbatical project in India, preferably, in her native Karala. During these discussions I suggested that she might consider doing a study on the Fields School that I had spoken to her about in past years. I had attended the Fields School during the first eight years of my schooling. She knew that I was proud of the Fields School, perhaps, most importantly, because it was founded by my grandfather, the man who had the greatest influence on my life and his brother.

One day Malathi said to me, "I have decided on my

sabbatical project. I am going to do a study of the Fields School." I was elated about the decision and promised to assist her in any way she thought me to be useful.

In early spring, prior to the 1998-1999 school year, Malathi contacted as many of the students and teachers who attended the Fields School as possible by letter. Accompanied her letter was a letter from me to people who know me. Subsequently, she contacted in person most of the students who attended the school and two persons who had taught at the school. I traveled with her on travelogues to Boston, Los Angeles, Chicago, New Orleans, Florida and Alabama where she interviewed each of these students and teachers separately.

Although primarily the work and research for this project was done by Malathi, she sometimes called me her "co-researcher." I certainly was her enthusiastic supporter. In her autograph for me in the second copy of her "Sabbatical Report," after keeping the first copy for herself, she writes: "This would not have been possible without you."

It is probably obvious to the reader that I could say much more about Malathi Karuven Sandhu and "The Fields School, - A Black School Without Failures." Suffice that I refrain from saying any more and present her "Sabbatical Leave Report that was submitted to NAU May 1999.

THE FIELDS SCHOOL

A Case Study of a School in Rural Alabama which served a Community of African American children from 1933-1949.

Sabbatical Leave Report Compiled by Malathi K. Sandhu, Ph.D. and Edited with Commentary by Uriah J. Fields

… a mass movement among African-Americans must be credited as primarily responsible for the creation of public school systems in the South in the aftermath of the Civil War. (Fultz, 1996; p. 145).

…it was during the period 1870-1885 that segregated, dual systems of education were formally established in former slaveholding states. (Fultz, 1996; p. 146)."

Beginning in the later 1880s, however, and continuing on a virtually uninterrupted upward slope into the 1940s separate education in those southern states that maintained de jure segregation became maliciously unequal. (Fultz, 1996; p. 146)."

INTRODUCTION

Many small, segregated schools which served African American children existed in the rural south during the period of the two decades from the early 1930s through the later 1940s. The Fields School, which was the object of this case study, was just such a small school. It came into being through the efforts of the then elder Fields family members. Recognizing the need for a school in close proximity to the Fields community, they requested available funds from the Washington County Superintendent of Education to support this endeavor. At the time, the only available funding for schools for blacks in the area was in the form of payment of teacher salaries, and some private funding for oversight of these schools. As Anderson (1988) points out when speaking of public education in rural Alabama in the late 1920s,"…rural black southerners, living in a cash-short economy and virtually disenfranchised by the public school authorities, paid from their limited resources a tremendous private cost for their 'public' educations. (p. 161).

The building and its furniture and furnishings, books, and teaching materials, with a few exceptions, had to be supplied by the local community or the group requesting county or state support for a school. …African American families have a long-standing commitment to the education of their children. The testimony of former slaves reveals such a strong desire for literacy and book learning that they learned to read, write, and spell through subterfuge.

Following the Civil War, African American families saw education as the key to literacy, which they hoped would in turn assure African American children a life of freedom and prosperity. Fearless in the face of poverty and discrimination and sustained by a distinctive orientation toward learning, during Reconstruction African American parents in the South (at times in cooperation with the Freedman's Bureau) built a free school system. (McCready, 1996; pp. 163-164).

In the mid-1930s, African American educator and historian Carter G. Woodson coined the term 'miseducation' to describe the existing educational theories, practices, and their outcomes pertaining to the education of African Americans. He argued that Africa Americans were being socialized to absorb and value an European knowledge base, beliefs, attitudes, customs, and behaviors. He proposed improvement in the quality of education for blacks, but did not really suggest different educations for blacks and whites. He did propose that …a true education for African Americans would not be controlled by others or teach them to serve the oppressors. Instead, it would be controlled by African Americans and would accomplish the following: it would equip African Americans to earn a living; it would allow them to manifest activities their authentic selves shaped by their traditional African cultures and histories and the social, political and economic conditions in the United States; finally, it would help African Americans develop into valuable contributing members of the community who will be empowered to shape its positive development. (Okazawa-Rey, 1996; pp. 297-298).

Whether or not the patriarchs and matriarchs of the various branches of the Fields family were aware of Woodson's proposals, their efforts certainly moved them in directions advocated by his work, as the findings of this study will show. They were aware that literacy was a tool for social change and provided protection against economic exploitation, and that education as a tool for attaining economic power and engendering a sense of personal significance and self-worth. They were confident that sending their children to an African American and community-controlled school would serve their children well.

THE PURPOSE OF THIS STUDY

The qualitative research study was undertaken so as

to profile the Fields School, a public elementary school which existed in the rural hamlet of Sunflower in Washington County, Alabama, between 1933 and 1949 and served a community of African Americans. An attempt was made by the researcher to identify the efforts that brought the school into being, to study the physical environment of the school, the curriculum taught, the teachers who served and their teaching methods and qualifications, the students who attended and their subsequent achievements and successes in coping with life in the world at large.

Research Questions Addressed in this Study

1) Did students/teachers who attended the Fields School regard their experiences as largely positive and successful?

2) What was the success rate for identified former students in terms of completing high school, college, entering professions and careers, etc.?

3) How did the school experiences of the Fields family members support the family's expectations and vice versa, how did nuclear family units support the school's operation?

4) What parts, if any, of the Fields School experience could be described as negative or weak, and why were they viewed in this way?

5) What agency and/or individuals provided administrative oversight for the operation for the school?

6) Under what circumstances was the school phased out?

METHOD

SUBJECTS

Of a group of about 35 students who had attended the Fields School, 26 former students were interviewed in person by the researcher. The 26 students interviewed had attended the school from a minimum of one academic year to up to eight academic years (for the eight grades, one through eight, which the school offered).

Of the four teachers who taught at the Fields School, two former teachers were interviewed who had taught at the school during its last three years of existence.

All former students and the two teachers who were interviewed belonged to the Fields family. These family connections over three generations are depicted in Table1 in a modified 'family tree' format.

This depiction includes only the male children of Benjamin Fields, Sr., and their offspring who resided in the hamlet of Sunflower, Alabama, where the Fields School itself was located.

DATA COLLECTION MEASURES USED

Two interview protocols were developed with a view to addressing the research questions formulated above. Twenty-one questions were developed as part of the interview protocol for former students of the Fields School. It was estimated in the pre-testing of this interview protocol, that it would take approximately one hour to administer.

Table 1

Fields Family Tree and Fields School students

(Listings from left to right and top to bottom by order of birth)

1. Benjamin Fields, Sr.

(born 1862)

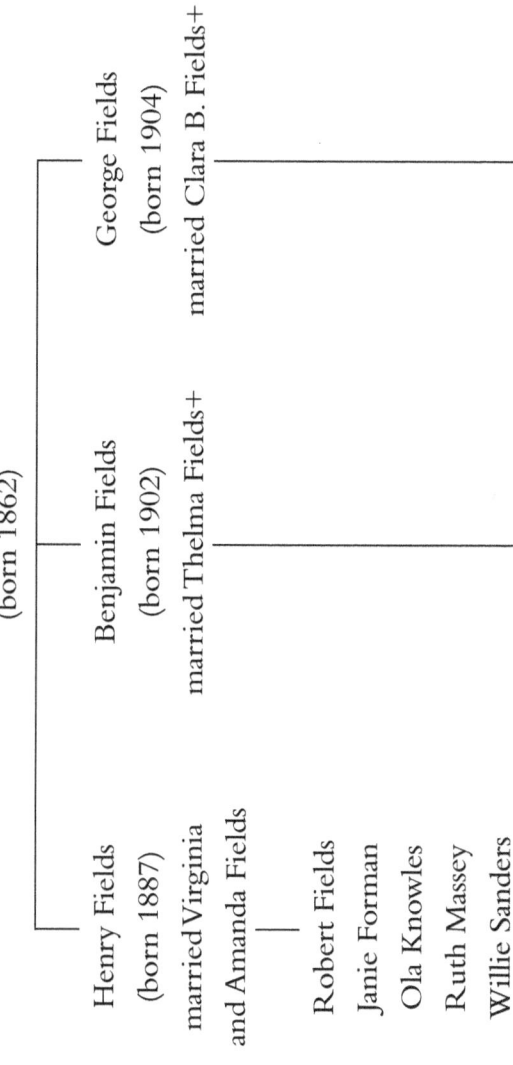

George Fields
(born 1904)

married Clara B. Fields+

Benjamin Fields
(born 1902)

married Thelma Fields+

Henry Fields
(born 1887)

married Virginia
and Amanda Fields

Robert Fields
Janie Forman
Ola Knowles
Ruth Massey
Willie Sanders

Henrietta Cooper★

Irving Fields★
(married Sarah
Hester Colvin+)

George Fields, Jr.
(deceased as a child)

Benjamin Fields, Jr.★

Augusta James★

Julia Owens★

Mildred Bettis★

Joe Fields

Ella Mae Bettis

Robert Fields★

Norman Fields★

James Fields★

Maureen Beard★

Leo Frederick Fields★

Henry Fields (deceased)

Ella Wiley★

Loyal Fields (moved to
Chicago as an infant)

Gertrude Lang★

Pearlie Mae Holcombe★+

Uriah J. Fields★

David Fields★

Jonathan Fields★

Bessie Mae Nettles★

Mary Taylor★

2. Alex Field

Alex
Fields,Jr. | Lucile Steely | Annie Mae Woodyard | Slade Fields | Martin Fields | Aileen F. House

Frankie F.
Smith★

Slade Milton
Fields

Woodyard
Hazel Tools★

Maxine
Berry★

Mary
Woodyard
Trotter★

John Alex
Woodyard

Annie Mae
Brown

Italicized and bolded names include students who attended the Fields School

★ indicates subjects interviewed by this study

+ Fields School teachers

The teachers interview consisted of twenty-two questions, and it was estimated that this instrument would take approximately an hour and a half to administer.

A background information sheet, to be completed by former students, was also developed to provide information including the subjects' dates of birth, years of school attendance, education and degrees earned, occupations, and careers pursued.

PROCEDURES

Each potential participant in the study was initially contacted by mail, indicating the researcher's interest in conducting this project, asking the cooperation of each subject, and soliciting by mail the participant's written permission and available times for a face-to-face interview. A second letter was sent to each potential subject informing each of the interviewer's scheduled time in the local community of each individual. The third contact with each subject was made by phone to set up the actual time for the personal interview. In some cases, more phone calls were necessary to confirm or modify as scheduled interview time.

Written communication with each potential subject was initiated in Spring 1998. Personal interviews were conducted between June 16 and October 13, 1998.

Each interview was conducted in person by the researcher with individual subjects typically in each subject's home in any available quiet area. Interview locations included living and dining areas, kitchens, and studies in homes. Four interview locations were other than in subjects homes. In one case, a subject was interviewed in the living room of her cousin's home (her cousin also being a participant in the study), as this was the most convenient location identified by the subject who was traveling daily to another distant location.

In another case, an interview was conducted in the office of the subject, again, at her request.

In two other instances, interviews were conducted in the hotel room of the researcher who had traveled to a conference in Louisiana expressly for the purpose of interviewing these two subjects.

In all cases, the interviewer and the subject were the only individuals present during the interview. The researcher asked for and, in all cases, was given permission to use a tape recorder during the interview. The researcher also kept detailed notes during each interview which, in review, were a very accurate record of the audiotape version of each interview. Following completion of each interview each subjects was asked to complete the background interview questionnaire which typically took each individual about five to ten minutes to complete.

Interviews were conducted by the researcher in seven states, Alabama, Arizona, California, Illinois, Louisiana, Massachusetts, and new York.

When the researcher visited Chatom Alabama, the county seat of Washington County, she visited the Board of Education offices and asked permission to study and copy available records pertaining to the Fields Schools and other schools in the county. She was able to examine and copy all relevant material from the Board of Education record of board meeting minutes for the time period extended from 1933 through 1949. These minutes, while very brief in most cases, included such information as the names of Negro teachers on the county/state payroll, the differential pay status of white and negro teachers, the initially different school terms for white and negro students, and the name of the appointed supervisor for the negro schools in the county. The information so gathered from the Board of Education minutes served to confirm and verify data provided by individual subjects during interviews conducted by the researcher, and information contained in the literature about education in the rural south during the 1930s and 1940s. Individual participants in the research study provided the researcher with treasured artifacts such as photographs of teachers and former students of the Fields School, a copy of family birth listings, and a grade report of one of the students. Copies of these were made and the originals returned to their owners.

The interviewer transcribed each taped interview before conducting an analysis of responses given.

Transcription of the audiotaped interviews took approximately five hours for each interview to be completed, and thus involved up to 150 hours of the researches time.

Summary of Findings of the Study

Interview Data from Former Fields School Students & Teachers

The data presented in this section were gathered from interviews conducted with 26 former students of the Fields School and two of their former teachers, Sarah Hester Colvin (later Fields), and Pearlie Mae Fields (Holcombe). See Table 2 for a listing of subjects interviewed by birth Table 2

Student Named	Birth Yr.	Yrs. Attended	Teacher (s)
Henrietta Cooper	1918	3	Clara Fields
Eileen F. House	1921	7	Clara Fields
Ella Wiley	1922	3	Clara Fields
Irving Fields	1924	6	Clara Fields
Benjamin Fields	1925	6	Clara Fields
Gertrude F. Lang	1926	8	Clara Fields
Julia F. Owens	1926	8	Clara Fields

Mary Woodyard Trotter	1927	8	Clara Fields
Joe Fields	1928	8	Clara Fields
Pearlie Mae Holcombe	1928	8	Clara Fields
Ella Mae Bettis	1929	8	Clara Fields
Uriah J. Fields	1930	8	Clara Fields
Robert Fields	1931	8	Clara Fields, Thelma Fields
David Fields	1932	7	Clara Fields, Thelma Fields
Norman Fields	1932	8	Clara Fields, Thelma Fields
Augusta James	1933	7	Clara Fields
James Fields	1933	8	Clara Fields, Thelma Fields, Sarah Hester Colvin, Pearlie Mae Fields
Jonathan Fields	1934	8	Clara Fields, Thelma Fields, Sarah Hester Colvin, Pearlie Mae Fields
Maureen Beard	1935	8	All four Fields School teachers
Bessie Mae Nettles	1936	7	All four Fields School teachers
Mildred Bettis	1936	7	All four Fields School teachers
Frankie Fields Smith	1937	8	Thelma Fields, Sarah Hester Colvin, Pearlie Mae Fields

Hazel Tooks	1939	4	Thelma Fields, Sarah Hester Colvin, Pearlie Mae Fields
Mary F. Taylor	1940	4	Thelma Fields, Sarah Hester Colvin, Pearlie Mae Fields
Maxine Berry	1941	2	Pearlie Mae Fields
Leo Frederick Fields	1942	1	Pearlie Mae Fields

Subjects attending the Fields School by Birth Year Categories, Years of Attendance, and Teachers year categories supplied by each individual, the years that each attended the school and their teachers during that time. In some cases exact dates of school attendance were provided but in other cases, these could not be provided by some subjects. In these instances, the researcher resorted to questioning these subjects about who had attended school with the individual, who had finished school with them, or started school just before the individual in question started. Such probing did often trigger memories of approximate dates of attendance, and were also pegged to teachers who had taught individual students.

THE ESTABLISHING OF THE FIELDS SCHOOL

The Fields School started operating on September 21, 1933, initiated by the efforts of Benjamin Fields, Sr. and Alex Fields, grandfathers to many of the students who attended, and the parents of many of the students, Henry, Benjamin, and George Fields.

The school came into being because there were many young children in the family who needed to be educated and the nearest public school for African American children in Sunflower was located 3 to 4 miles distant from the Fields community. There was no busing available for black children at the time. Transportation to the nearest black school called Red Hill or Sunflower #2 would have been difficult for the families to arrange for the large number of Fields children who would be attending. In fact, one of the older students who later attended the Fields School spoke of having to walk the many miles to Red Hill School. Another subject stated that her father would not allow her to attend Red Hill as it was too far a distance to walk.

The County Superintendent of Education, Mr. T. J. Pearson, was approached by the older members of the Fields family and apparently gave consent for the Fields School to be established. The minutes of the County Board of Education do not acknowledge the establishing of the school, but in the Board meeting minutes of November 28, 1933, Clara Fields, the first teacher at the Fields School, is listed among the negro teachers "elected" by the Board for the 1933–34 session

Students Attending Fields School.

Table 1 shows that all of the subjects, that is former students, attending the Fields School were members of the Fields families, most being first and second cousins to each other. While most of the subjects interviewed had started school at age five, one student stated that she had started at age three years, and there were some who had started at age seven or even later (as was the case of those who had started when the school first started).

In discussing their impressions of fellow students at the Fields School, a majority of responses focused on the fact that they were all related by blood, and were family members (n=11). More than a third of the responses pertained to how well they got along together and how much fun they had together (n=9). An equal number of responses (n=9 focused on the fact that fellow students were striving to improve themselves and learn. These findings are presented in Table 3.

Table 3
Frequency Counts for Impressions of Fellow Students

Impressions of Fellow Students	Frequency
All related by blood; family	11
Got along with each other; had fun	9
Striving to improve selves, learn	9
Helped each other, shared	3
Nobody got into trouble	3
Got together in age groupings	3
Don't remember much	2

*Total frequencies do not add to 26; some Ss gave more than one answer

Over half the subjects (n=14) interviewed graduated from 8th. grade at the Fields School.

Three former students completed 7[th.] grade at the school. Eight students were unable to complete the eight grade of schooling offered at the Fields school because the school was closed in 1949 due to lack of minimum enrollment required by the County Board of Education. One of the older students who attended the school for only three years, upon completing 7th. grade, went to work as she needed to do this, and obtained her GED many years later.

Most of the students (n=19) who attended the Fields School attended and graduated from McIntosh Union High School, located about 8 miles from Sunflower, Alabama.

Four students attended Prestwick High School (about 12 miles from Sunflower, Alabama) after leaving the Fields School, and three attended a boarding school, Presbyterian Boarding School in another county (Wilcox) and graduated from there.

When asked whether the Fields School experience had prepared them for their subsequent schooling experiences 25 subjects said that it had, with 23 stating that they were very well prepared for their next school experience.

One subject stated that he was not well prepared for his next schooling experience, indicating that they had not been exposed to very much while at the Fields School.

When former students were asked whether the Fields School experience had prepared them for other life experiences which followed their high school experience, 24 subject indicated that it had and two stated that it had not. When further questioned about whether they felt in any way hampered by the Fields School experience again, a large majority (n=22) stated that they did not, but to the contrary felt they were "blessed" with having a school so close by, with all family attending, and proof of that was that they were able to compete very successfully with other students after leaving the Fields School.

Four former students stated that they did feel hampered by the Fields School experience, two because of the social limitations of being with only family members, one because of the lack of science lab facilities, and one because of the generally limited exposure to academics at the school.

FIELDS SCHOOL TEACHERS

Table 1, in addition to portraying a modified family tree for the Fields family, also provides the names of three of the Fields School teachers.

Table 4
Fields School Teachers and their individual Terms of Service*

First Teacher:	Mrs. Clara B. Fields
	Hired November 28, 1933
	Years taught: 1933-1943**
Second Teacher	Mrs. Thelma Fields
	Years taught: 1943-46**
Third Teacher	Mrs. Sarah Hester Colvin (later Fields)
	Years taught: 1946-47

Fourth Teacher	Mrs. Pearlie Mae Fields (later Holcombe)
	Years taught: 1947-49**

Source: Mrs.
Pearlie Mae Holcombe
** Years taught represent academic years teachers.

In chronological order these are: Clara B. Fields who was married to George Fields, Thelma Fields who was married to Benjamin Fields and Pearlie Mae Holcombe who was first a student at the Fields School and subsequently served as the fourth teacher during the last two years of the school's existence. The third teacher was Sarah Hester Colvin Fields, who married Irving Fields, and who served between the terms of Thelma Fields and Pearlie Mae Holcombe.

See Table 4 for a listing of the four Fields School teachers and the terms they served.

In responding to a question pertaining to the teachers the subjects had at the Fields School the preponderance of responses was positive and made reference to the teachers' focus on the students' learning (n=13), how good, dedicated, and academically strong the teachers were (n-11), how loving the teachers were (n=11), and the creativity of the teachers in the activities they conducted n=5). These findings are presented in Table 5

Table 5
Frequency Count for Students'
Impressions of Teachers

Impressions of Teachers	Frequency
Focused on students' learning	13
Good, dedicated teachers; academically strong	11
Loving teachers	11
Creativity in activities teachers conducted	5
Stern disciplinarian	4
Fostered sense of self-worth	1
Good role model	1
Teacher was fun	1
Teachers taught all grades	1
Teachers always had parental support	1
Physical characteristics of teacher noted	1

*Total frequencies do not add to 26; some Ss gave more than one answer

When questioned about the guidance techniques and disciplinary measures used by the teachers at the Fields School, a large number of students noted that their teachers would use physical punishment, if that was needed, including using a strap (n=17). Most also stated that the threat of parents finding out that there had been a discipline problem at school, and administering their own and usually more severe punishment was very real (n=12). Interestingly, a large number of students also noted there were no discipline problems at school as students knew the teachers' expectations and were familiar with school routines (n=17). These findings are presented in Table 6.

Table 6
Frequency Count for Typical Guidance & Discipline used by Teachers

Guidance & Discipline used by Teachers	Frequency
Physical punishment, if needed	17
No serious discipline problems at school	17
Threat of parents knowing & discipline at home	12
Talked to students	5
Created expectation for self-expression	3
Made to stand in corner	2
Teacher was role model	1

*Total frequencies do not add to 26; some Ss gave more than one answer

The two teachers who were interviewed indicated neither had used physical punishment with their students, but added that they had dealt with few, if any, serious discipline problems. One of the teachers did state that parents would have dealt with any serious problems if they had occurred. In discussing their preparation to teach at the Fields School, both teachers interviewed indicated that at the time, because of the general shortage of teachers, one did not have to complete a bachelor's degree in order to teach. One had to possess a "D" certificate to teach, and was given a certain period of time to complete the requirements for a "C" certificate. Mrs. Holcombe had completed high school and almost two years of college when she first started teaching. She had immediately enrolled in college upon completing high school, had gone to summer school, and attended college the following fall semester. She was all of 18 years of age when she started teaching high school. She continued attending college in the summers until she completed her requirements for a bachelor's degree. Mrs. Colvin Fields had completed one year of college when she started teaching at the Fields School.

One of the former students describing her mother's (Mrs. Clara B. Fields) preparation as the first teacher at the Fields School, said, "She was a good teacher. It seemed like she knew her subject matter." She went on to describe her mother's struggle to qualify as a teacher. Clara Fields graduated from Dunbar High School in 1939 and then attended summer school at the Mobile Branch School in Mobile, Alabama. Sometimes, in the Spring session she attended college in Montgomery, and also attended night classes in Mobile. There were times when mother and daughter attended classes together, both completing degrees at the same time in Elementary Education.

Another former student speaking of Mrs. Clara Fields, her only teacher at the school, stated that, "The Fields School was ahead of its time because of the teacher. She wasn't just on the payroll, she gave it her all. She went beyond the call of duty." There were other such strong testimonials to the skill and dedication of Clara Fields and all the other Fields School teachers from almost all of the subjects interviewed for this study.

DESCRIPTIONS OF THE PHYSICAL SETTING OF THE SCHOOL

Located in the Fields community in close proximity to the homes of the various Fields families, former students described the school building as "the little brown house" because it was painted a brownish red color. It was a wooden building with a tin roof, built as a home, not a school. The home had belonged to an aunt and uncle of many of the subjects who had moved to Chicago. Classes were usually held in two rooms, the living room and dining room which opened into each other an could be converted into one large classroom. The building also had a kitchen, front porch, screened back porch, and was heated by a wood-burning stove in the winter. Indoor furniture included benches, a writing desk about 12 feet in length, a few chairs, a chalkboard and some tables. Many students and both teachers recall holding their writing materials in their laps while they worked. The furniture and furnishings had been made by the parents of the children who attended the school.

An outdoor area, approximately 30 feet by 70 feet, had been cleared for a playground. There was a basketball court, a fields for track, and an area where students played softball. There were separate outhouses that served as toilets for the boys and girls. A few students recalled that there were crape myrtle and magnolia bushes in the front yard. There was no running water or electricity. Instead, a hand-operated pump provided water outdoors, and kerosene lamps provided lighting when needed. Former students recall collecting wood during recess periods for the wood stove.

When asked what there was an abundance of at the school, most subjects cited the positive emotional climate of the school environment. There responses to this question are presented in Table 7. As is apparent, more than half the subjects (n=17) cited the love, caring, and concern among the students, and nearly half the group (n=10 cited the teachers' love and caring for the students.

Table 7
Frequency Count of Responses Indicating What was in Abundance at School

What was in abundance at school	Frequency
Love, caring, concern among students	17
Teachers' love and caring for students	10
All were friends at school	5
Lack of abundance of material things	5
Adequate supply of material things	3
Sharing	2
Enjoyment of each other & activities	2
Discipline	1

*Total frequencies do not add to 26; some Ss gave more than one answer

Conversely, when asked what was in short supply at the Fields School, the majority of responses of former students centered on the lack of material things such as books and reference materials (n=10), and other supplies, furniture, and furnishing (n=9). And yet, almost one quarter (n=7) responded to this question by stating that they had the basics (n=7). These findings are presented in Table 8.

Table 8
Frequency Count for Things in Short Supply at School

Things in short supply at school	Frequency
Books, reference materials	10
Other supplies, furniture, and furnishings	9
Had the basics	7
Learning activities	1
More students in each grade	1
Lunch program though school years	1
School building	1
Money for personal needed	1

*Total frequencies do not add to the 26; some Ss gave more than one answer

When asked more specific questions about whether there were enough books and supplies at the school, who provided these, and what students had to bring from home, 11 former students responded that there were not enough books per student, while nine responded that there were enough books.

A large majority of former students (n=23) indicated that parents had to provide paper and pencils and other supplies, and a small number (n=5) indicated that teachers furnished students with supplies.

The two teachers interviewed also described the limitations of the physical environment at the Fields School. One described them as "very poor conditions," and a "makeshift" school, crudely furnished with home-made furniture.

When former students were questioned about the one thing they would change about the Fields School if they could, the largest number (n=10) responded that they would change nothing, as the school was good, and they had had the best that was available at the time (see Table 9). A little less than one-quarter of the sample responded that they would have wanted more amenities including a larger facility, running water, better furniture, a better heating system and hot lunches served at school.

Table 9

Frequency Count for What they would Change about the School

One thing to change about school, if could	Frequency
Nothing, it was good, best available	10
More amenities (e.g., larger facility, running water, etc.)	8
Equipment, teaching materials, books	7

Wider exposure to more people (other than family)	4
Textbooks, more and better	1
Longer lunchtime	1

*Total frequencies do not add to 26; some Ss gave more than one answer

The two teachers' response to this question of what they would change about the school were quite practical and realistic. One suggested that more teachers would have helped to provide individual attention to students, but the space would not have accommodated more teachers and separate classrooms. The other former teacher responded that there were many things she would like to have changed but could not. She would have wanted better lighting, and a "good desk" but "had no control of those things."

FIELDS SCHOOL CURRICULUM

When the subjects were asked to describe the curriculum taught at the school, all of them noted that they were provided with a basic academic curriculum that was common to the entire state of Alabama. Also noted were the art curriculum, games and sports such as track, softball and basketball played during recess, singing and music, extracurricular activities such as exercise programs, and special events such as Christmas, May Day, Thanksgiving, plate suppers held after school for fund raising, and a yearly Field Day.

A grade report card for one of the subjects replicated in Figures 1 and 2 indicates that in 1940, the subjects taught in 8th, grade included Reading, Math, Spelling, Health, English, History, Geography, and Science. Letter grades were assigned by the teacher in each of these subjects and students were also evaluated by a letter grade in the area of "Conduct."

It should be noted in passing, that during the war years, for a period of about three years, the school received food commodities that enabled the providing of hot lunches for the students attending during this period. A cook was hired to prepare these meals, and most students spoke very positively about this experience and the availability of foods that may have otherwise been somewhat scarce in their diets, e.g., peanut butter, cheese, powder eggs and baked potatoes. Except for this short period when lunch was provided at school, most students who attended either brought their lunches or went home for lunch during the hour that was allocated for this activity.

Former students indicated that part of their time at school was devoted to maintaining their physical environment as indicated in Table 10. Most (n=23) indicated that they were responsible for keeping their school room clean. Ten subjects mentioned that they were responsible for maintaining the school grounds, a smaller number (n=8) indicated that they had to collect and bring in wood to keep the wood stove supplied during winter. An even smaller number (n=6) stated that they were responsible for assisting in such daily school routines as taking out the trash, passing out coats, and helping serve food.

Washington County Schools	Reporting Periods

Washington County Schools

Fields School

Julia Fields

Name of Pupil

Grade Eight Session Beginning

Clara B. Fields

Name of Teacher

Certificate of Promotion

This is certify that the above pupil has completed the work as outlined in the course of study for the Eight grade and is hereby promoted to the Ninth Grade Clara B. Fields Principal Given This 10th day of April 1941

Signature of Parents

1 Mr. & Mrs. Ben Fields, Jr.
2   Ben Fields, Jr.
3   Ben Fields, Jr.
4   Ben Fields, Jr.
5   Ben Fields, Jr.
6   Ben Fields, Jr.
7   Ben Fields, Jr.

Reporting Periods

1 2 3 4 5 6 7 8

Days Absence

Unexcused

Absence

Times Tardy

	Reporting Periods
Conduct	C C C C C B B
Reading	B B B B+ B+ A A
Math	B B B B+ B A A
Spelling	A A A A A A A
Health	C C C B+ B B B
English	B B B+ B+ B+ B B
History	C C C C C C+ B+
Geography	C C C C C C+ B
Science	C C C C C C+ B+

A- Excellent

B- Good

C- Fair

D- Poor

F- Failure

I -Incomplete

Figures 1 and 2 Front and Back of a Grade Report Card for an 8th grade Fields School Student from September 1940

Table 10

Frequency Count for How Learning and Work were Combined at School

Work Performed at School	Frequency
Keep schoolroom clean	23
Maintain school grounds	10
Bring in wood to keep wood heater going	8
Routines such as taking out trash, passing our coats, etc.	6
Decorate school room	1
Water plants	1
Don't remember	1

*Total frequencies do not add to 26; some Ss gave more than one answer

When questioned about the most important lessons learned at the Fields School, one third of the subjects (n=9) responded that they learned cooperation, sharing and getting along with others and an almost equal number (n=8) cited the strong curriculum taught at the school. These results are presented in Table 11.

Table 11
Frequency Count for Important Lessons
Learned at Fields School

Important Lessons Learned at School	Frequency
Cooperation, sharing, getting along with others	9
Curriculum taught	8
Achieving & setting goals, maintaining standards	4
Respect for others	4
School & Home closely related	4
Comfort with teachers	3
Self-worth	3
Respect for God, Religious education received	3
Value of community	2
Being responsible for self and others	2
Helping younger students	2
Togetherness, feeling close to others, being loved	2
Honesty, fairness	1

*Total frequencies do not add to 26, some Ss gave more than one answer

In a related question, subjects were asked what important life values they had learned at the Fields School.

These findings are summarized in Table 12.

Most former students (n=12) again noted the values

of being cooperative, sharing and getting along with each other.

Other values noted were unspecified ones that nevertheless were important for later success in Life (n=10).

Table 12
Frequency Count for Life Values Leaned at the Fields School

Life Values Learned at School	Frequency
Being cooperative, sharing, getting along	12
General values for later success in life	10
Work ethic; work hard for what you want,	8
Responsibility for one's own behavior,	8
Respect for one another and oneself	7
Integrity; being honest	7
Being prepared for school, being on time, etc.	4
Daily morning devotion	4
Developed feelings of self-worth	2
Sense of purpose in life	1
Obedience	1

*Total frequencies do not add to 26; some Ss gave more than one answer

To summarize the findings of this section, responses to a question about the most stirring memory that subjects have of their experiences in the

Table 13
Frequency Count for Most Stirring Memory of School

Most stirring Memory of School	Frequency Count★
All family members who attended	16
Teachers who were family/caring & concern	8
All students lived in same geographical area	2
How the school came into being	2
Learned so much at the school	2
Walking to school on winter mornings	2
In class by self	1
Spelling Bee every Friday	1
Playing games during recess	1
Going to local high school to demonstrate math	1
Parents involved in school	1
Death of teacher's son	1

★Total frequencies do not add to 26; some Ss gave more than one answer

Fields School are presented in Table 13. A majority (n=16) responded that it was the fact that all who attended were family members. A second most frequently given response (n=8) pertained to the fact that their teachers were family members who displayed considerable caring and concern for the students. Other responses included that they all lived in the same geographical area, that they were impressed with how the school had come into being, they had a Spelling Bee every Friday, one student was in a grade all by herself, that Fields School students went to McIntosh High School to demonstrate math skills to older students.

In a related question, when asked what they would like children of today to experience that they had experienced at the Fields School, the most frequently given positive response (n-12) pertained to the caring, concern, and general effectiveness of their teachers. The next most frequently given positive response (n=7) pertained to the family atmosphere of love, respect, and support that pervaded the schooling experience.

Five subjects noted the very strong math teaching they received as students. Not all subjects felt they would want their own children or kinfolks to have experiences similar to

Table 14
Frequency Count for What would want for Young Children today to Experience of Fields School

Would want children today to have similar experience	Frequency Count*
YES Caring, concern effectiveness of teachers	12
Family atmosphere of love, respect, & support	7

Strong math teaching received	5
Individual attention received	3
Community/ parent interest in school & schooling	3
Routines practiced at school, including at recess	3
Values imparted at school, including religious curriculum	2
School being within walking distance of home	1
Discipline at school	1
Learned from older students	1
NO Would want exposure to broader curriculum	5
Very small number of students at each grade level	1
Repetition of subject matter at various grade levels	1

*Total frequencies do not add to 26; some Ss gave more than one answer.

What they had at the Fields School (n=7). The most frequently given reason for this was they would want exposure to a much broader curriculum (n=5).

Table13 summarizes these responses.

Background Information on Former Fields School Students

The data presented in this section were gathered from the Background information questionnaire completed by each subject who was a former student of the Fields School.

Of the 26 former students interviewed, 16 are women and 10 are men.

Current Residence of Subjects

The 26 former students of the Fields School currently reside in communities, towns, and cities of varying sizes. A few (n=9) had returned to settle in the hamlet of Sunflower, Alabama, or a nearby community of Calvert, Alabama, both of which have populations of less than 1,000 persons.

Almost equal number of subjects have settled in the greater metropolitan areas of Boston, Chicago, Los Angeles, New York and Mobile.

The remainder of the subjects currently reside in communities varying in size between these two extremes. Table 15 summarizes the current residential patterns (in 1998), of the subjects interviewed.

Table 15
Frequency Count for Current Patterns of Residence

Size of Residential Areas	No. of Subject
Rural, unincorporated, under 1,000	9
Rural, incorporated under 1,000	1
Population 1,000-2,500	1
5,000-10-000	3
250,000 and over	2
Greater Metro areas (Boston, LA., N.Y., Chicago, Mobile)	10
Total	26

EDUCATION COMPLETED BY SUBJECTS

Table 16 summarizes the educational achievemens of this sample of subjects and is broken down by gender of the subjects.

Over three-quarters (n-20) of these sample had completed a bachelor's degree.

Of these, over half (n-12), had completed some graduate work.

Eight subjects had master's degrees, and one had earned doctorate.

One individual had been awarded an honorary doctorate.

Table 16
Frequency Count for Education
Completed by Gender

Education Completed	Male	Female	Total
High School	1	1	2
Some College	1	3	4
Bachelor's Degree	3	5	8
Some Graduate Work	2	1	3
Master's degeree	2	6	8
Doctoral Degree	1	1★	2★

★Honorary Doctorate

OCCUPATIONS AND CAREERS OF SUBJECTS

Table 17 summarizes information regarding the occupations of this sample of subjects, by gender. Almost half the sample (n=12) had pursued lifelong careers as teachers. This group of teachers averaged 29 years each of teaching experience in public school systems. Of this group of teachers, 11 subjects were female. Other individuals in this group had pursued careers in public service (country and state government, including administrative positions), had worked for private companies, have served as an attorney, and in the military.

Table 17
Frequency Count for Occupations/Careers by Gender

Occupation/Career	Male	Female	Total
Education	1	11	12
Private Company	2	3	5
Government/ Administration	3	1	4
Self-employed	2	0	2
Military	1	0	1
Labor Representative	1	0	1
Law	0	1	1
Total	10	16	26

Although several individuals in this group have retired from services, many continue to work (n=10), and some in newly chosen fields.

HIGHEST INCOME EARNED BY SUBJECTS

Table 18 summaries the highest income earned by the subjects participating in this study. About one-third of the group (n=9) had listed incomes over $45,000 as the highest they had earned. Of these, six had earned over $50,000 in the course of their careers.

In reviewing the data presented in this section pertaining to background information on the subjects interviewed, it is apparent that this group of individuals represented a high degree of success in educational and career achievements.

All had graduated from high school, many had attended college, several had entered a variety of professions, and all had held long-term employment throughout their lives.

Table18
Frequency Count for Highest Income Earned by Gender

Highest Income Earned	Male	Female	Total
Below $10,000	0	1	1
$10,000 to $20,000	0	8	8
$20,001 to $30,000	2	2	4
$30,001 to $40,000	2	24	
$40,001 to $50,000	3	0	3
Over $50,000	3	3	6
Total	10	16	26

DISCUSSION OF RESEARCH QUESTIONS

1) Did students/teachers who attended the Fields School regard their experiences as largely positive and successful?

The answer to this question is a resounding "yes." In responding to a question asking what subjects would like the world to know about the Fields School, half (n=13) responded that it was a great school and prepared them for life, and almost a third (n-8) responded that as a small black school in a

Table 19
Frequency Count for Student Responses (=26) to What the World Should Know about the Fields School

What the World should know about Fields School	Frequency
Great school, prepared me for life	13
Small black school in a small black town achieved much	8
Value of the human spirit enhancing life	6
Value of sharing	6
Value of cooperation & extended family	5
Teachers gave their best	5
Our own family school	1
Not anything	1
Don't know	1

*Total frequencies do not add to 26; some Ss gave more than one answer.

small town, it achieved much. Other responses included that it demonstrated the value of the human spirit enhancing life (n=6), and the value of sharing (n=6).

These findings are presented in Table19. The two teachers also responded very positively to this question, one of them saying, "We did the best we could with nothing. We tried and accomplished something." The other teacher included in her response that "The Fields School, even though it existed many years ago, was A-rated."

2) What was the success rate for identified former students in terms of completing high school, college, entering professions and careers?

As is apparent from the tables and narative summarizing the educational and occupational achievements, and income earned by the subjects of this study, the answer to this question would have to be that all of these individuals have been highly successful in their lives. Not only did they all complete high school, but most had completed at least a four-year college degree, and over one-third had taken graduate work.

In addition to this many "firsts" are represented among the individuals in this group - "first black judge appointed to the State of Alabama" (who also passed the Alabama Bar in 1967), "first black woman to work in the tax assessor's office in Chatom," "voted Teacher of the Year at a Middle School (an integrated school), and only the second black teacher who taught English at an integrated elementary school," "first black woman to attend Eastern Oregon College and earn a master's degree," and so on.

As one of the former teachers described the quality of education that she provided at the Fields School, and the success achieved by her former students, "I provided very good wholesome activities to instill in them (the students) to keep searching for better things.

They were able to do that. They became Lawyers, teachers, nurses."

3) How did the school experiences of the Fields family members support the family's expectations and vice versa, how did nuclear family units support the schools operations?

Some students portrayed the school as "just an extension of the family." The values taught at school were those learned in the family as well. Of course, most of the children attending were taught by an aunt, a mother, a sister, and sister-in-law, so that there was continuity between the experiences of home and school. Bible verses were taught and memorized at school, and supported what one student referred to as the Fields family's strong orientation to church-going.

Another student stated that the life values she learned at the Fields School were her family's values. The work chores performed by the students at school paralleled the responsibilities they had in their own families and in the community.

Many unsolicited examples of how the family supported the school operations were provided by most of the former students interviewed. One referred to how the school came into being when he said, "A family, parents concerned about the educational system that made no provision for blacks. So, your parents had to take the initative." And they did, in providing a school building, building furniture for the school from their own meager resources, and even providing the teachers for the school from among family members. Parents supervised children at home in their completion of homework assignments. They were quick to discipline children at home for infractions committed at school. Parents bought school supplies and teacher supplies that the county did not provide.

4) What parts, if any, of the Fields School experience could be described as negative or weak, and why were these viewed in this way?

Former student were aware that access to schooling for blacks in the rural South was limited in the 1930s and 1940s. They mentioned that school busing was unavailable for black children but was available for white children at the time. One stated, "With segregation as it was, to see the buses pass by the end of the road and you couldn't ride them.

Five southern states in 1929-30 provided publicly funding transportation for 439,732 white students, 17 percent of their total enrollments, but transported only 4,970 black students, one-half of 1 percent of those enrolled. Long distances to be traveled on foot to dilapidated, under-supplied facilities only compounded the disadvantges of short school terms, overcrowded conditions, lack of voice in control and administration, and other aspects of enforced inferiority perpetuated by dual systems. (Fultz, 1996; p. 147).

This was why a school in the community was needed. Even though another school, Sunflower #2, Red Hill, in the hamlet of there was Sunflower, Alabama, it would have been too far for young childen to have walked the distance of three or four miles to get there.

The limitations of the physical environment have been mentioned by many students and the two teachers interviewed. The school itself was located in the living and dining rooms of a home. So, the setting was not designed for a school. The classroom space has been described as small and poorly furnished. One student wished the classrooms "would have been larger." There were benches but no desks and written work often had to be done in one's lap. There was no indoor plumbing or electricity in the school building. One teacher described the setting as an "impoverished school."

When the teachers were asked to describe other schools where they taught either before they came to the Fields School, or after they left the Fields School, both teachers mentioned the larger schools with more amenities and better facilities they experienced subsequent to their leaving the Fields School. "McIntosh was a cut above. There were more students, more teachers, a regular school building... They had a piano there. And had music and assemblies. It wes a big difference."

The other teacher recalled, "...they had better facilities, more equipment, a copy machine, a gym for activities. More state books, phonographs, filmstrip projectors, science equipment such as microscopes..." However, the Fields School was not atypical for rural schools in the South which served African American students.

Well into the 1930and 1940s, substantial numbers of African-American youth attended rural one- and two-teacher "schools" that lacked desks, blackboards, sufficient textbooks, and other basic necessities of quality education. (Flutz, 1996; p. 147).

In terms of the curriculum taught, while most of the students perceive their schooling experience as being strong, a few noted the limitations of the science curriculum because they lacked laboratory facilities and specimens, and tended to focus on natural and general science.

When questioned about the adequacy of books and supplies available to them at school, some of the former students remarked on the fact that books and reference materials were in short supply.

This was especially true in the early days of the school.

Some subjects also noted that "The state had the books but they were not being issued to the blacks. Usually, we got used books after they had been used by some other (white) schools." So. very often, textbooks were "worn out" by the time they arrived at the school, with missing pages, and marked up during prior use.

Three students mentioned the limited social exposures that the Fields School with its population of extended family members provided. One student stated, "I wished those first eight years, I could have been with other than family folks. I didn't mix with other children till I was 15 years old....I just wished I could have mixed early socially." Another subject speculated that this may have been the reason why she felt "inferior" when she went to college, even though while attending the Fields School, she had felt like she was "the cat's pajamas." This latter subject had also been the only student in her grade at the Fields School. Another former student mentioned that because "We were all kinfolk, therefore there were no boy friends or girl friends" at the Fields School.

One former student and a former teacher at the Fields School did point out the limiations of a one-teacher school. "One teacher had to teach all the grades.

She did the best she could. We got a pretty good background. English and math could have been taught better. Most teachers specialize." Both teachers interviewed for this project were just beginning their teaching careers when they were at the Fields School. A multigrade teaching assignment must have been a challenge for these beginning teachers.

To summarize, when former students of the Fields School were asked about the most negative experience they had at the Fields School, most (n-18) seated that they had experienced no serious problems that they could remember. When the two former teachers were asked the same question, one stated that she did not have any negative experiences at the Fields School, but looked forward to the next day at school. The other teacher indicated, "The conditions under which I had to teach. The kids not having things," adding, "I had been to a better school."

5) What agency and/or individuals provided administrative oversight for the operation of the school?

The Alabama State Department of Education was the authority regulating education in the state at the time when the Fields Schools was in operation. On a local level, the County Board of Education located in Chatom, Alabama, was the agency which provided oversight for the operation of Schools within Washington County.

As was apparent from board minutes housed in the County Board of Education building in Chatom, the county Board of Education met on a monthly basis to consider matters pertaining to education and schooling within its jurisdiction. The County Superintendent of Education, Mr. T. J. Pearson, is described by former teachers and students of the Fields School as having oversight over all schools in the county, but was not known to have visited any black school during the period in which the Fields School existed. Instead, a Jeanes worker/teacher, Mrs. Ruby Callaway, was the liaison between the Board of Education and black schools.

Jeanes Workers in rural Alabama exercised a special function, "These rural workers, virtually assistant superintendents, were accepted and put to work by Alabama, Arkansas, Georgia, Kentucky,...." (Bullock, 1967; p.135).

They were commonly called Jeanes supervisors, and had multiple tasks which included "community improvement centered around the home" (Bullock, 1967; p. 136). The Jeanes teacher's work also dealt with the heart of the instructional program in rural negro schools. "In their duties as supervisors they helped teachers develop their lesson plans" (Bullock, 1967; p. 137). One of the Fields School teachers interviewed confirmed the supervisory role played by the Jeanes worker, Mrs. Ruby Callaway, and the fact that the white superinendent did not ever visit the school during its years of operation.

6) Under what circumstances was the Fields School phased out?

The Fields School was closed on September 8, 1949, although no record exists in the Board of Education minutes to indicate a formal closing of the school.

Former students and teachers of the school indicate that it was closed due to lack of the minimum enrollment. It appears that there would have been only 10 students attending in the fall term of 1949, and the requirement to keep the school open was a minimum of 15 students. Most of the students who would have attended went on to attend either Sunflower #2, Red Hill School or McIntosh Union, which by that time included grades one through twelve.

The last teacher at the Fields School continued to teach in Washington County, Alabama at Koenton High School before moving on to other county public schools for an extended career as a teacher.

Conclusions

It is obvious from the data presented in the foregoing sections that the Fields School, despite its modest physical surroundings and meager furnishings, was a highly successful enterprise in terms of providing an Educational foundation for its attendees. One might speculate on the factors that contributed to the remarkable success of Fields School students given the fact that their families were burdened by poverty, minority group status, and the social and political climate and practices of the state of Alabama and the Union in the period extending from the early 1930s through the late 1940s.

Nieto (1996) points to the role of "cultural congruence" in the successful education of minority students. That is, "...the teacher acts as a father, brother, and friend to students; he holds high expectations for them; students learn to develop collective responsibility for one another....; and there is a commitment to extending the life of 'the family.'" (p.147)

She also indicates that "...African American families of academically successful children provide extended family and community support, provide racial socialization and act as teachers in the home." (p 275)

By racial socialization she meant developing in children a sense of pride in their own race as a means of preparing children to face obstacles in the larger society. In the case of Fields School students, they were all members of a large extended family who lived in the community surrounding the school. The former students all noted in their interviews the caring and love in the school setting that emanated from their teachers, but were also experienced among the siblings and cousins. Although the Fields did not foster an "us" against "them" mentality in their dealings with whites, there was a strong sense of racial pride and a history of real accomplishments in the elders of this family. They were people who made things happen, lived in that part of Sunflower where no other black families lived, and who knew of even though they were not fully acknowledged by their white cousins and antecedents who lived in the same community. Grandfather Benjamin, born into slavery acquired large land holdings and worked these with his sons so that he and his sons would not have to work for whites.

Greene (1978) speaks of the importance for effective student learning of countering official definitions, interpretations, and namings that are rendered by a depersonalized society such as our own with the development of a "wide-awakeness associated with full attention to life and its requirements." (p. 152).

In active attention, there is always an effort to carry out a plan in a space where there are others…a shared world that places tasks before each one who plays a deliberate part…In a domain of human expectations and responses (where) individuals find themselves moved to make a recognizable mark…In the course of acting in the light of what is taken to be relevant, the individual tests himself or herself, tests his or her potency." (Greene 1978; p. 152).

Situations must exist or be created that will permit

the release of individual capacities, that will permit persons to identify themselves.

To identify the self is, in a sense, to understand one's preferences; to understand them is to be able to reflect upon them in the light of some standard, some set of values, some norm…One has to be with others, reflectively…in a space one knows is a shared space and one has to care. (Greene 1978; p. 153).

If such situation exist, persons can develop autonomy and become persons who …keep their promises, … listen to others' viewpoints…respond to requests for help,…do their work as decently as they can and rely upon self-validation.

Gadsen (1991) reminds us that Literacy acquisition is affected by a variety of factors, such as cultural and social contexts for acquiring and using literacy, motivation for learning, and functions of literacy learning. Access to literacy in this framework denotes the conditions that allow an individual---minority or majority…to participate in literate activities such as reading writing, and communicating…conditions that foster the acquisition and development of values and abilities and that increase not only the involvement of minorities and others in society but also feelings of self-worth and capability to achieve personal goals. Literacy can be said, then, to result in a way of thinking and integrating one's thoughts, experiences, and knowledge into the learning process…freeing the learner from intellectual subservience, fear, and feelings of inadequacy. (Gadsen, 1991; p. 191).

The Fields family and school appear to have inculcated in its members both a strong sense of autonomy and self-definition, which propelled them to achieve measurable successes in their educational, occupational, and life pursuits. All of them seem to have avoided the pitfall of "logofixion", or becoming damaged by the expectations and words of the larger society that tend to cast minority group members in stereotypical roles of society's victims or society's romanticized noble ones (Peshkin, 1997). They were and are able to live in two worlds, with a minimum of conflict, and gained cultural competence in a black and white world, in the community of their origin, and the society at large.

The overwhelming success of the Fields School, despite the limitations of physical settings, furnishings, and available materials and books, represents a triumph of this unusual family over difficult circumstances. The story of the school, while interesting and informative, is really the story of the Fields family, since the school was an extension of the family's commitment to its children. The story of the family is yet to be written.

References Cited

Anderson, J. D. (1988). The education of blacks in the south, 1860-1935. NC: University of North Carolina Press.

Bullock, H. A. (1967. A history of negro education in the south from 1619 to the present. MA: Harvard University Press.

Fields, Uriah J. (2006). Grandpa Benjamin. Baltimore: Publish America.

Fields, Uriah. J. (2007). The Saint Troubadour: Speaking and Singing Truth and Love. Baltimore: Publish America.

Flutz, Michael. (1996). Dual systems of education. In F. Jones-Wilson C. Asbury, M. Okazawa-Rey, D. K. Anderson, S. Jacobs and M. Fultz (Eds.), Encyclopedia of African-American education. CN: Greenwood Press, 1996.

Gasden, V. (1991). Trying one more time! Gaining and regaining access to literacy in African-American youth and adults. In M. Foster (Ed.), Readings on equal education. Volume 11, Qualitative investigations into schools and schooling. NY: AMS Press, Inc., 1991.

Greene, M. (1978. Landscapes of learning. NY: Teaches College Press.

McCready, Lance. (1996). African-American family influence on schooling. In F. Jones-Wilson et al. (Eds.) <u>Encyclopedia of African-American education</u>. CN: Greenwood Press.

Nieto, S. (1996). <u>Affirming diversity: The sociopolitical context of multicultural education</u>. NY: Longman, 2nd ed.

Okazawa-Rey, M. Miseducation. (1996). In F. Jones-Wilson, et al. (Eds.) <u>Encyclopedia of African-American education</u>. CN: Greenwood Press.

Peshkin, Alan. (1997). <u>Places of memory; Whiteman's choices and Native American communities</u>. NJ: Lawrence Erlbaum.

OTHER REFERENCES

Clark, F. G. (1934). <u>The control of state-supported teacher-training programs for Negroes</u>. NY: Bureau of Publications, Teachers College, Columbia University.

Colson, E. M. (1940). <u>Analysis of the specific references to Negroes in selected curricula for the education of teachers</u>.

Submitted in partial fulfillment of the requirements for the degree of Doctor of Philosophy in the Faculty of Philosophy, Columbia University. NY: Bureau of Publications, Teachers College, Columbia University.

Foster, M. (1997). <u>Black teachers on teaching</u>. NY: The New Press.

Lomawaima, K. T. (1994). They called it Prairie Light: <u>The story of Chilocco Indian School</u>. NB: University of Nebraska Press.

Mihesuah, D.A. (1993). Cultivating the Rosebuds: <u>The education of women at the Cerokee Female Seminary, 1851-1909</u>. IL: University of Illinois Press.

Mohraz, J. J. (1979). <u>The separate problem: Case studies of black education in the north, 1800-1930</u>, CN: Greenwood Press.

Wieder, Alan. (1997). Race and education: Narrative essays, oral histories, and documentary photography. NY: Peter Lang.

Appendix

A Brief History of the Fields School

In the "Acknowledgments" of Uriah J. Fields' book, "Grandpa Benjamin," (published in 2006), he writes:

…special thanks to the late {Malathi Karuven Sandhu}* who during a sabbatical leave from Northern Arizona University where she was a professor made a study of the Fields} School that Grandfather had established in the early nineteen thirties in the hamlet where he was born and lived all the years of his life. Her research on the {Fields} School was a contributing factor in helping me to make the decision to write about Grandfather Benjamin.** (p. 6).

This "Appendix" contains the verbatim information on the Fields School found in "Grandpa Benjamin," except for the replacement of the fictional names with true names. These true names will appear in brackets.

The excerpt is as follows:

"The school age children living in the {Fields} Community…had to travel - most of them walking - four miles each way to get to {Sunflower # 2 School} that was also called the Red Hill School. Because of the distance Children living in the {Fields} Community had to walk their absentee rate

was high and it was not because they were being home schooled. Grandpa and the parents of their school age children living in the {Fields} Community were concerned about the distance these children had to travel in order to attend school.

Early in 1932 Grandpa and his three sons, (Henry Harold, Benjamin F. Jr., and George} and their wives, my mother {Amanda, Aunt Thelma and Aunt Clara B.}, respectively and Great Uncle {Alexander} and his wife Great Aunt {Missouri} their oldest son (Alex, Jr.} and his wife {Phyllis} and their middle daughter {Lucile} and her husband {John H.} attended a meeting held at Grandpa's home for the expressed purpose of determining the feasibility of establishing a school in the {Fields} Community. These thirteen persons, including Aunt {Thelma} and Aunt {Clara} who were teaching at other schools in {Washington} County. {Henry Harold, Benjamin F., Jr., George, Aunt Thelma and Aunt Clara} were selected to serve on a fact-finding committee that would obtain information on how to proceed with establishing a school in the {Fields} Community.

Two weeks later the same persons who had attended

the first meeting attended a second meeting.

They decided that the {Fields} Community should petition Superintendent of Education {T. J. Pearson} and the Board of Education of {Washington} County with the request that a school be established in the {Fields} Community. Grandpa, Great Uncle {Alexander} and Aunt {Clara} were selected to contact the Superintendent and request a meeting with the Board of Education for the purpose of submitting an application for the establishment of a school in the {Fields} Community.

Subsequently they submitted a proposal to the Board of Education with a request that a school be established in the {Fields} Community that would begin its operation in October 1933. This was the month that other schools opened that were attended by black children in {Washington} County. Schools attended by white children opened a month earlier. This practice of opening schools that black children attended a month later than those attended by white students had existed since the end of the Reconstruction period. Some years schools attended by blacks also closed a month earlier than schools attended by whites. Black children were kept out of school a month after white children began school so they could help harvest the crops and black schools were closed a month before white schools so black children could help plant and cultivate crops. At this time, however, the school year for black students was one month rather than two months shorter than the school year for white students.

Present for what would prove to be a significant meeting were the representatives from the {Fields}

Community, the Suprientendent of schools, the representatives from the Board of Education and two {Washington} County government officials. After some discussion on establishing a school in the {Fields} Community Grandpa offered to provide a house, free of Charge to {Washington} County, that could be used as a school house. The Superintendent of Education and the other officials present were taken by surprise. Later the Superintendent and some of the other representatives commended Grandpa for his generosity and with limited discussion that followed these officials on the Superintendent's recommendation authorized that a school be established in the {Fields} Community. The Superintendent promised to hire a teacher for the school who would be paid $34.00 a month. This was about one-half the amount paid beginning white teachers. All black teachers in {Washington }County received less pay than white teachers. The Superintendent also stated that some used books, used chairs and a used teachers desk, all currently being used at the white {Chatom} School, would be transferred to the new school that will be established in the {Fields} Community.

Gleefully he announced that all these items being removed from the {Chatom} School would be replaced with new ones, to the satisfaction, if not delight, of other white people participating in the meeting. After observing the response from the white representatives, without specifying the materials, the Supreinendent said that certain teaching materials could be transferred from a white Washington County school to the new school.★

The school opened in late October 1933, one month later than other black schools. Aunt {Clara} who was already teaching at the (Sunflower #2, Red Hill} School was hired to be the teacher at the new school and her new salary was two dollars a month more than she had received in the past. She had three years of teaching experience. Aunt {Clara} was the wife of Grandpa's youngest son {George}. Representatives of the {Fields} Community decided that the school would be named the Benjamin F. {Fields} School. Grandpa, perhaps out of his modesty, objected to the school being named after him. After further deliberation it was agreed by the representatives of the {Fields} Community and approved by officials of the {Washington} County Board of Education that the school would be named the {Fields} School. Everyone in the {Fields} Community realized that the school had been named after, for, and in honor of {Benjamin F. Fields, Sr.,}

*Sources:

Collaborative recollections of three subjects and their ages who attended the Fields School the first year it was established; Henrietta Cooper 15; Ella Wiley 13 and Gertrude 7. even though his name had not been included in the official name of the school.

Even though my parents, {Henry Harold}, his first wife (deceased) and his second wife {Amanda had five children, Uncle {Benjamn F. Jr.,} and Aunt {Thelma had five children, Great uncle {Alex} had one child and his daughter {Annie Mae} had two children, a total of thirteen children, who would be the students eligible to attend the new school, no one was more excited about the new school than seventy-one year old Grandpa who, allow me to add, was as vigorous and energetic as any adult in the {Fields}Community.

Grandpa said that he had promised himself to do all that was in his power to establish a School in the {Fields} Community. He kept his promise. His dream had been realized.

On the Saturday before the Monday when the school would open the thirteen young persons who would be the first students to attend the school were all present to register. Their parents, most of their siblings, including some who were too young to attend school, including myself who would have to wait two years before I could be enrolled in the school, some other community people and Grandpa came to the house that would soon be a schoolhouse to celebrate the opening of the new school. There were jubilation, singing, rejoicing, and dancing, even though the adults present would not admit that they were dancing. Some of them considered dancing to be sinful, hence an undersiable activity for God-fearing people to engage. Eating, talking and laughter were also on that day's menu. A person would probably be correct if he said that Grandpa was the keynote speaker that day. Like President Abraham Lincoln who spoke just three minutes when he delivered the Gettysburg Address, Grandpa spoke about the same length of of time. He talked about how the school came into existence and thanked everyone who had helped to make the dream of having a school in the {Fields} Community a reality. He mentioned how pleased he was with the way the community people had turned out for the celebration that marked the opening of the new school. Then he praised Aunt {Clara} who had been selected to be the first teacher of the school and made a pledge to her, on behalf of the community, to support her in making the school a good school, as he put it,"a top-notch school." After stating how happy he was, he predicted that the {Fields} School will produce students who will be as knowledgeable and as well educated as the students attending the County's white schools.

Before Aunt {Clara} could respond Cousin {Anne Mae}, I supposed having been inspired by Gandpa's remarks as were everyone present, began singing the old spiritual "Great Day!"These are the words of the chorus that were sung over and over again by the choiring audience who joined in the singing with Cousin {Annie Mae}:

Great day!

Great day the righteous are marching!

Great day!

God's going to build up the Zion walls.

Following the singing Aunt {Clara} thanked Grandpa who she credited with being the person who was most responsible for establishing the school. She expressed thanks to a number of people, calling some of them by name, who had helped in establishing the school. She thanked everyone who had played a part in selecting her to be the teacher for the school and pledged to do her very best to be the kind of teacher that the students, parents and people in the {Fields} Community will be proud of.After welcoming everyone who had come to celebrate the school opening Aunt {Clara} said "This little brown house, where we are gathered, has been donated by Grandpa Benjamin to be our schoolhouse and it has been named the {Fields}

School." Subsequently, most people in the {Fields} Community called the school the "Little Brown House." Several other persons made remarks and all who spoke praise Grandpa for the contribution that he made in establishing the school.

The Little Brown House had three rooms. Two of the rooms appeared to be one room when the wide double doors that separated them were opened.

There were a kitchen, a hall way, a front porch and a pantry. About twenty feet from the house there was a garage. Originally, this house had been built by Grandpa for his daughter {Julia} who married and moved to Chicago. The {Fields} School that opened in November of 1933 closed in May of 1949. About thirty-five students attended the school during these sixteen years it was in operation. Like myself, some of the students were students at this school for eight years. The school never had an enrollment that exceeded fifteen students. While attending the school two students died, one at the age of eleven and another at the age of fifteen. Eighty percent of the students who attended the {Fields} School graduated from college. Four of them earned master's degrees, one a law degree and two earned doctoral degrees. Nearly a third of them taught school on an average of twenty-nine years before retiring. The last teacher at the {Fields} School was my sister {Pearlie Mae} who had enrolled as a student at the {Fields} School the first year that it was opened.

Grandpa was eighty-seven years old the year the school closed and even though he was very ill at the time he came to the school's closing event.

He expressed satisfaction that the school had been

in the {Fields} Community when it was most needed. He recalled a prediction he had made on the day the school opened when he said, "This school will produce students who will be as well educated as students attending the white schools in {Washington} County." He felt that his prediction had come true. He had lived to see students of that school achieve and be productive. Looking into the eyes of {Pearlie Mae,} he said, "You are a top-notch teacher."

Then he asked everyone present, even though he was unable to do so himself, to stand and give {Pearlie Mae } a big round of applause. Everyone except Grandpa stood and enthusiastically applauded {Pearlie Mae}. Grandpa had a smile on his face and an awe-gripping glow in his eyes that conveyed the message that he had come full-circle and had helped to bridge the past with the future. It was apparent to all present for that school closing event that Grandpa was saying farewell, not just to the closing of the school, but to his descendants.

the school closed because, in the judgment of the members of the Board of Education of {Washington} County, there were not enough students attending the school to justify keeping it open. As Grandpa had observed "the school had been there when it was most needed." To that, I , an alumnus of the school can say "Amen."

Approximately a year and three months later, on December 15, 1950, Grandpa died. Four months before his death I sent Grandpa a letter. At that time, I was in the Army and the soldiers in my regiment, indeed the entire division of which I was a part, were on high military alert...the unofficial word was that we would receive orders at any moment to go to to fight in Korea. Unable to get a furlough to visit Grandpa, I wrote him a letter that I sent to my sister Gertrude. I asked her to read it to Grandpa as many times as he wanted to hear her read it. I knew how much Grandpa enjoyed listening to Gertrude read. With this prose poem I closed my letter to Grandpa:

To love the earth you know, for
greater knowing;
To lose the life you have, for
full life;
To leave the friends you love for
heavenly loving and angelic fellowship;
To find a land more sweet than home
and more awesome than earth.
Behold! A wind is rising and rivers
are flowing;
Your soul too is rising and flowing;
You are communing with the wind
and the rivers.
You, the wind and the rivers are one.

Farewell Grandpa!
Your Grandson,

Uriah
(From "Grandpa Benjamin", p. 151)

ACKNOWLEDGMENTS

So many people influenced this volume that it would be impossible to mention them all. But I must acknowledge with gratitude the names of the indispensable contributors to this production.

I acknowledge with gratitude administrators of the College of Education at Northern Arizona University who approved researching the Fields School as a Sabbatical leave project.

I acknowledge with gratitude the authors cited in this volume, namely, F. G. Anderson, H. A. Bullock, Uriah J. Fields, Michael Flutz, V. Gadsen, M. Greene, Lance McCready, S. Nieto and M. Okazawa-Rey and Alan Peshkin.

I acknowledge with gratitude the twenty-six former students of the Fields School, including two teachers, one who had been a students, who were interviewed for this case study. Each was interviewed separately.

I acknowledge with gratitude Benjamin F. Fields, Sr., most often referred to in this study as Grandpa or Grandpa Benjamin. More than anyone else he was responsible for establishing the Fields School alone with his brother Alex who supported him.

I acknowledge with gratitude my mother and father, Amanda Fields and Henry Harold Fields, who instilled within me and my siblings, mostly by their examples, a desire to be responsible and to love unconditionally.

I acknowledge with gratitude, Clara B. Fields, the first and only teacher of the Fields Schools for ten years.

She was admired by her students who attribute their success to her being an effective teacher.

My greatest ackowledgement and gratitude from the depth of my heart go to Malathi Karuven Sandhu, the chief researcher for this case study that is the heart of this book. I intimately and warmly experienced her for a quarter of a century. She, above all else, encouraged me to write this book and in fidelity I dedicate this book to her.

About the Author

Uriah J. Fields, born in Sunflower, Alabama, is a clergyman and author of "Inside The Montgomery Bus Boycott - My Personal Story" and "The Saint Troubadour - Speaking and Singing Truth and Love." He was a founder and original secretary of the Montgomery Improvement Association that provided strategic leadership for the Montgomery Bus Boycott. For thirty years he was the director of a human development center in California. He served as a Chaplain's Assistant during the Korean War. He lives in Virginia.

www.ingramcontent.com/pod-product-compliance
Lightning Source LLC
Chambersburg PA
CBHW021233280526
45784CB00005B/2079